T0194187

EVERYBODY WANTS YOUR MONEY

ANNA L. MONTESSI, PETER M. MONTESSI

authorHOUSE®

AuthorHouse™
1663 Liberty Drive
Bloomington, IN 47403
www.authorhouse.com
Phone: 1 (800) 839-8640

Published by AuthorHouse   03/13/2020

ISBN: 978-1-7283-4707-3 (sc)
ISBN: 978-1-7283-4706-6 (e)

Library of Congress Control Number: 2020902868

Print information available on the last page.

Anna L. Montessi
Everybody wants your money: a guidebook to keeping it / Anna L.
Montessi; Peter M. Montessi; Amy Jordan, Graphic Artist.
1. Finance, Personal
2. Saving and Investment
3. Consumer Education

HG179. m66 2020
332.024'008'35
QBI00-460

CONTENTS

AUTHORS' ACKNOWLEDGMENTS

This book represents the collaborative efforts of many people.

We owe special thanks to family, friends, colleagues and critics. They have shaped our thinking about the topics covered. To all those to whom we are in debt, we extend our deepest appreciation.

We are particularly grateful for the advice and encouragement reeived from the following persons: Harold Jasper, Sue Runyard, Barry Barnett, Jonathan Jackson, Sharon Brock, Susan Chan, Ernest Fierro and Kristine Berg.

There is, however, one person without whom this book would have been impossible, Judith L. Rothman. Her patience, good humor, knowledge and editorial assistance helped bring this book to completion

Finally, we dedicate this book to our parents.

Anna L. Montessi
Peter M. Montessi

To learn one subject really well
You first must break it down
Into pebble-sized concepts.
Only then can you build
A mountain of knowledge.

—Roberto Alvarez—

Samples, Examples and Questionnaires

AN INTRODUCTION
TO THE READER

Who was this guidebook written for? This guidebook was written for any person handling household accounts. You may be single, married, head of a large family, divorced, a single parent, and/or living with roommates. Whatever your household situation may be, this guidebook was written for you.

What will you learn? You will learn how to organize and manage your household finances and how to save money, even on your current income. You will learn how to create a personal financial plan, and, ultimately, gain financial freedom.

This book is not a "get-rich-quick" fix. It is a guide to show you how to live successfully within your means. It presents the keys to living well on your current income. These are:

BE DETERMINED to live a better life and set goals.

EVALUATE your goals.

ASSESS and understand your current financial position.

REASSESS you financial position one month from today, one year and ten years from today.

The process of DETERMINATION, EVALUATION, ASSESSMENT and REASSESSMENT will help you attain your goals. This guidebook will provide the most basic tools to help you through the process.

Take another look at the title: **EVERYBODY WANTS YOUR MONEY.** The "Everybody" we refer to is family, friends, government, schools, advertisers, merchants, retailers, salespeople, strangers, etc. Our goal is to help you understand that every dollar you spend should be based upon your own sound, conscious decisions. You will learn that **YOU** are in total control of your money. Awareness and control will help combat financial stress.

There are a few conditions you must meet to use this book effectively:

> You must have an **income**.
>
> You must **recognize** that you need to improve your current financial position.
>
> You must be **honest** with yourself regarding your spending habits and other issues related to your finances.
>
> You must have the **ability and time** to follow the procedures set forth in each chapter.
>
> You must have the **desire** to change existing habits.

We applaud you for buying this book. You have taken the first step toward achieving **financial freedom. CONGRATULATIONS!**

HOW TO USE THIS GUIDEBOOK FOR MANAGING AND KEEPING YOUR INCOME

Use this book as a lesson-plan guide for yourself, or to teach family and friends. You can use a chapter or a section in the chapter as a lesson. To assist you in the learning process, you will find:

Samples, Examples and Questionnaires

Following the Table of Contents is a list of the Samples, Examples and Questionnaires, showing the assigned Chapter and page number for each. You may want to refer to these frequently. The Samples illustrate how a document or form will appear. The Examples are demonstrations used to show you how to fill out the forms. The Questionnaires are for you to fill out.

Money Guidelines

The following pages contain the Money Guidelines. These Guidelines are the Rules to remember and follow while using this book. Real life is full of difficult and unexpected money situations and financial emergencies. By practicing these Guidelines, you will find that overcoming money problems come easier.

MONEY GUIDELINES

Below is a list of simple rules. Although you may already be acquainted with most of them, they will serve as a reminder when you enter problem situations.

T   Never loan your money to anyone. It will not be returned to you. This is a loss, not only of your money, but of a friend or relationship with someone.

T   Never trust someone to hold your money, unless it is a professional, such as a broker or banker. They will never take better care of it than you. You also run the risk of never seeing the entire amount again.

T   Value what you have. About once a month, look around you. Appreciate where you are now. Look at where you were one month ago, one year ago, and five years ago. Notice how far you have progressed. This process will help you keep your situation in perspective.

T   Reevaluate your goals. The items that money could buy one year ago may cost more or less now in terms of cash, time and responsibility. Have your goals changed? How?

T   Never spend your money in a hurry. When you are pressured or in a rush, you can make mistakes, such as over spending or buying the wrong product or service.

T   Reserve a day to shop on a day when you are not working. Do not stop in the grocery, hardware store, department store or a discount store on your way home from work. Wait for the weekend. Also, do not shop for food when you are hungry.

T   Research before you buy.

T   Know that with each new purchase comes added responsibilities.

T   Use Cash – for your weekly allowance.

T   Use Checks – whenever possible.

T   Use Credit Cards for:

> Auto Repairs
> Home Repairs
> Emergencies

T   Never use a Credit Card Cash Advance

T   Do not allow your emotions determine your spending habits. Loneliness, guilt, anger, excitement and eagerness will prevent you from making good purchasing decisions.

T   Change spending **HABITS** into spending **DECISIONS.**

CHAPTER 1

Goals

This chapter will teach you how to create and organize financial goals. You will learn that it is important to write down what you want to achieve. This simple process keeps you focused. Your written goals will be used to develop a plan of action. An example is included showing a family walking through the steps in order to illustrate this process.

Everyone has goals. Most goals require some amount of money, whether it is for lessons, classes, or any type of interactive education. There are desires to own a doll or toy, a piece of electronic equipment, a computer, luxury items, repairs for household appliances, clothes, a larger apartment, owning a home or car. Or even bigger goals like owning a business, becoming financially independent or retiring early. It is important to make a written record of every goal you have now.

You have probably been told that millions of dollars will not buy happiness. I think you should be the judge of that.

It is important to determine what all of your goals are, no matter their size. Ideas will be flowing. Write all the goals down, so that none are overlooked. Date the pages in which the goals are listed.

Study 1

Randy worked for a defense manufacturing company as a supervisor for the shipping and receiving department. He was single and lived at home with his parents. He paid a modest rent of $250.00 a month. His basic expenses were low. He had many goals in mind, but was not able to achieve them.

For the first time, he wrote down all of his goals. He wanted to own a house, own a business as a disc jockey and own the special equipment needed to run and operate his business. But, he never saved any money toward his goals. He always felt that they were too far out of reach.

Upon examining his spending habits, he discovered he was paying twice as much for his truck, than for the rent. He remedied that right away by purchasing a truck with much smaller monthly payments. Randy enjoyed dating and frequently picked up the tab when he went out with his friends. He spent more money during the weekends than for the entire week.

So, he cut back. Instead of going out Friday AND Saturday of every weekend, he went out one night per weekend. He alternated between weekends, those that he would pay for the evening out, and the other, his friends would.

As a result, during the first month, he saved $500.00. He took half of his savings, $250.00 and purchased some of the equipment he needed to begin his "dream" business. He received his first job as a disc jockey and was paid $50.00. That $50.00 was placed back into savings. He was on his way to achieving his goals.

#1 - Example - Goal Form

Name	Goal	Estimated Cost	Details/Notes
Ava	Vacation	$312.00	Trip to the mountains in Aug. 3 days in a cabin.
Ava, Joe	Car	$18,000.00	Need something reliable, safe & comfortable for 5 people
Sandra	College Education	$28,000.00	Nothing saved and three years to go.
Sandra	Used Car	$10,000.00	Only 2 years saved.
Calvin	Personal Computer	$1000.00	This is important. I could use it for school.
Little Joe	Dinosaur Doll	$12.95	This is important.
Ava, Joe, Sandra, Calvin, Little Joe	Color Television	$500.00	It would be nice to get rid of the old 17" and get something bigger.
Ava, Joe	Retirement	$1 million	We could live comfortably if we only had $1 million.
Ava, Joe, Sandra, Calvin, Little Joe	Dinners Out and Movies	$153.00	Family outings, when possible and affordable.

#1 Example Goal Form (above) shows that no goal is too large or too small. Everyone has hopes to acquire something that would improve the family or individual's way of life. Creating a basic outline, a road map can be make to meet some or all of these goals.

Notice the table does not include dates which these goals are to be met. The dates to achieve these goals will fluctuate as events occur, such as children growing up, job and career changes, want and desire changes, etc. A set deadline to meet the goal will cause unnecessary anxiety, especially if it is unrealistic for you.

Your listed financial goals need to be achievable and realistic. Although dreams can sometimes come true, usually they are outside of your immediate reach. Dreams can be so big that they may require the good luck of winning a lottery, or stumbling upon an unclaimed treasure. Chances of this happening are slim and you cannot count on this.

The example parents, Ava and Joe, will need to explain to their children that they will need to keep their goals within reason. They need to tell Calvin, for example, that buying a Tesla this year is not realistic. They need to explain to Little Joe that the dinosaur doll may have to wait. And they need to let Sandra know that a castle off of the coast of France just isn't going to happen with their family plan.

It is important to understand the difference between a dream and a goal.

It's great to dream! But, this current project is to create goals that the family can work on and begin to feel a sense of financial control and accomplishment.

It is interesting to note that when you discuss your goals with people, there is always someone who will tell you that you will not be able to achieve them. That you will fail. Don't EVER believe it. When family or friends share their goals with you, be as supportive of them as you would want them to be of you. This is the time to believe in yourself.

BASIC STEPS FOR GOAL CREATION AND COMPLETION

1. When you really want or desire something, it automatically comes to the forefront of your mind. You think about it over and over again. You begin to play different scenarios in your mind interacting with this goal. This is the very first stop to making your goal a reality.
2. The second step is to write down the goal(s). When you write the goal down, as a statement, it becomes more tangible. It has been placed upon a piece of paper that you can touch and feel. Instead of it being in your imagination, it now exists on paper. You will want to find a picture of your goal(s), especially if you are sharing them with your children.
3. The third step is to keep your written goal(s) near you so that you can read and re-read them often.

One suggestion is to keep it on top of the entire set of bills needing to be paid. Or in front of your ledger book. Then you will be sure to see those goals daily or weekly – and you will be reminded of them.

4. The fourth step is to create a holding place, using any type of concealable container to hold the coins and cash that you accumulate. (Later, you will put this in the bank). This object can be large or small. It can be a coffee can, a soda or water bottle, a shoe box or any container that can be hidden away as you build the cash. Label your container with your goal.

In **#1 Example Goal Form (p. 9)** there would be (9) nine individual containers. Each container could be alike, with a different label or each could be a different size, made of different materials, such as a glass jar, plastic bottle or small cardboard box. But, each container must have a label with the goal.

To complete this chapter:

1. Create your goals. List everything that comes to mind.
2. After the goals are written, prioritize them.
3. Estimate the cost or the amount of money you will need to meet the goals.
4. Establish the cash savings containers and label them with the goals you have written. No amount of money is too small to start.
5. Add coins and small bills to the cash containers whenever possible.

Once assembled, you will begin to develop plans to achieve those goals.

GOAL SUMMARY

It is essential that you use these steps to help you achieve your goals. You will begin to establish a new pattern in your thinking: **The Process of Saving for the Things You Want.** Some of these goals will be achieved very quickly. Others may take a lifetime. It doesn't matter how long it takes, the point is to begin NOW.

Save small amounts of money toward a small goal. The longest journey begins with a single step. The experience you gain while saving for the small goals will assist you greatly as you move toward the larger ones.

After writing your goals, you are ready to begin **Chapter 2 – Make a Plan.** You will learn how easy it can be to accomplish goals when you follow the steps.

CHAPTER 2

Make a Plan

In this chapter you will learn how to create a plan and look at the possible paths you can take. You will learn to write them out and view the steps as assignments. Then, you will organize those paths to develop a personal, step-by-step guide to achieve the goals you created in Chapter 1.

Creating a plan is the most crucial step toward making your financial goals a reality.

EXAMINE YOUR GOALS TO DEVELOP A PLAN

In #1 Example Goal Form, Little Joe requested a dinosaur doll. The family knows that they can purchase it for $21.95 at the toy store down the street. The family concentrates on how Little Joe will be able to earn the money to achieve this for himself.

Plan Suggestions to Earn the Necessary Money Include:

   T   Recycling plastic bottles and cans for coins.
   T   Work around the house performing tasks such as dusting furniture, folding laundry, making beds, etc.

T   Improve school grades – the parents may give a small financial reward.

T   Perform small jobs for neighbors.

When the entire family focuses on the one small goal and provides Little Joe with options to make the money needed to purchase this item, the process will take very little time. When the goal is achieved and the money has finally been saved, the entire family can share in the good feelings of Little Joe's achievement. It is important to hold on to this feeling and enjoy the experience.

To make the experience memorable, the family will go to the store with Little Joe and watch him make his selection. They will go through the checkout line with him, and after bringing the doll home, discuss the entire experience.

KEEP YOUR RECEIPT

Take an envelope and staple it permanently to the back of the goal sheet. Place the receipt inside of the envelope. Write on the goal sheet the date of the purchase and mark it off as completed! When young children are involved, using gold stars or stickers on the form is a good way to make their accomplishments stand out from the rest.

This will help you to establish the good habit ot retaining receipts. Always expect the unexpected and be prepared. If you keep your receipt, you may be eligible for repairs, rebates from manufacturers, exchange of merchandise, replacement through insurance, or possibly a tax deduction. Those little pieces of paper can be just as valuable as the item you purchased. The additional bonus you receive from this exercise is the personal sense of satisfaction when you can mark off the goal from the goal sheet as completed.

How long should you keep your receipts? That depends on why you will need to keep them.

1. If you are keeping receipts in case of a future return, then 30 days.
2. If it is due to a warranty, then the warranty will tell you. Some are good for only 30 days, while others are good for as long as two years.
3. If it is for a tax deduction, you will want to keep the receipt for seven years.
4. If it is for insurance purposes, such as flood, earthquake or other damages that could be inflicted to your home or personal belongings, then you will want to keep the receipts indefinitely.

ORGANIZE YOUR GOALS

The family in our example will want to concentrate on other goals on the list. It is time for them to adjust and examine the goal priorities.

In the following example, there are three completely different types of goals.

1. The one-time expense for a single item.

2. The recurring expense that may come up weekly, monthly or annually.
3. The extremely long-term goal that could take years to achieve.

We will now examine these items and learn how to handle them.

#2 Example Goal Organization

Name	Goal	Estimated Cost	Progress	Date Completed	Type of Goal
Little Joe	Dinosaur Doll	$21.95	Goal Accomplished	Feb. 1, 2001	One Time Purchase
Family	Color TV	$500.00	Saved $12.25. Made a plan. Need $487.75.		One Time Purchase
Calvin	Personal Computer	$1000.00			One Time Purchase
Sandra	Used Car	$10,000.00	Found Loan Rates from Bankrate.com		One Time Purchase
Ava, Joe	New Car	$18,000.00	Found Loan Rates from Bankrate.com		One Time Purchase
Sandra	College	$28,000.00			One Time Purchase
Family	Dinners Out or Movies	$153.00			Recurring
Ava, Joe	Vacation	$312.00			Recurring
Ava, Joe	Retirement	$1 Million			One Time Purchase

The example goals are arranged in order of the least expensive to the most expensive item. Notice the pattern in the far right column. The least expensive items are the one-time purchases. The recurring items, although the dollar figure is low, will occur month-after-month or year-after-year. When these figures are multiplied over 20 or 30 years, these items will (of course) cost the family more. The last, and most expensive item is long-term.

A one-time purchase is very simple. But, look at the range in prices. This example shows the smallest at $21.95 and the largest at $28,000. The more an item costs, the more time you will want to spend to make sure you are getting the best product or service for the money.

Each item from the Goal List will require its own Plan: the step-by-step instructions to achieve it. The same plan to acquire a dinosaur doll will not apply to purchasing a color television. Although the same principals apply, it will take longer to achieve and there will be more time, money and effort required.

#3 Example Plan To Acquire Color Tv With Remote Control

Questions & Answers

1. We wanted this and who will benefit?
    The entire family.
2. Who will work on this plan?
    The entire family.
3. How much will it cost?
    $500.00 (approx.)

4.   How much as been saved?
                     $12.25 (exactly)

5.   How much is still needed?
                     $487.75

Action Plan	Who Will Be Responsible?
1.	Sell the old black & white television
	Ava & Joe (Try selling on Ebay).
2.	Hold a yard sale
	Entire Family
3.	Cut back eating in restaurants
	Entire Family
4.	Local babysitting jobs
	Sandra (4 times)
5.	Neighborhood lawn care
	Calvin (4 times)
6.	Recycle bottles & cans
	Little Joe
7.	Save $25.00 per paycheck
	Ava & Joe

This example working plan requires everyone in the family to participate. Everyone wants the color television and the entire family will benefit from owning it. If each individual does their part, the goal to acquire the television will be achieved in a reasonable amount of time. But, if any one person does not follow through on the plan, it could take weeks or months longer to achieve.

While creating a plan to achieve a goal is the first step towards accomplishment, the plan must be put into motion. If you don't follow the plan, the goal will not be accomplished! You must focus your energy and time on performing every step. Don't let events and situations get in the way. There are a million excuses and reasons why you cannot accomplish your goals. DO NOT LET THIS STOP YOU. Be determined, no matter what the circumstances are. JUST DO IT!

To complete this chapter, create your plan and write down:

1. Who it is for?
2. Who will work on the plan in order to accomplish the goal?
3. What it will cost in terms of money?
4. How much money has already been saved?
5. How much money is still needed to meet that goal?
6. Next, write the assignments and the individuals that will be responsible for completing the tasks.

When you have finished this, you will have created a written plan that is ready to be acted upon.

PLAN SUMMARY

You learned in Chapter 1 – Goals to create and write your goals. In this chapter, you learned to organize and prioritize your goals. You learned to examine them in order to determine which would be the easiest and quickest to accomplish. Then, you organized that information on paper.

After completing all the assignments required for achieving the goal, you will be ready to begin the research needed to acquire your goal item. Chapter 3 – Research will provide you with the information you will need to perform the

CHAPTER 3

Research

This chapter will teach you methods for conducting research. Research, in this case is better known as shopping – and is the process of examining and comparing what you are trying to obtain. Price and quality comparison among products or services available and the location in which they are being offered is an information gathering process. The better informed you are before making the purchase, the better your decision will be when it comes time to making the purchase.

Study 2

Roger was recently divorced. He moved from the house he and his wife owned and rented a modest 1-bedroom apartment. He began to shop for furniture and electronic products at a large mall nearby. He was horrified to discover the prices were so high. He had not been shopping in years and did not realize what it cost to buy the things he needed. He came home that day without purchasing a single item.

Roger asked his new neighbors about the stores that would offer better deals. He was given several suggestions. He could shop at thrift stores, pawn shops, GoodWill and Salvation Army stores, used furniture and appliance stores or look on Ebay and Amazon.com. Another suggestion was to offer to purchase a store's floor model at a discount. Roger was also given catalogs by his neighbors. This provided him with the information regarding what the products would cost.

Prepared with this new information, Roger began to make phone calls to various shops in his area and made comparisons. At the end of two weeks, his apartment was furnished with appliances and a television. This was done at a fraction of what the cost would have been if he had purchased everything from the original store at the mall. Roger learned that by taking a little time to comparison shop, he was able to buy more with his money. It was worth the time he spent asking neighbors for advice and using the phone before walking into the stores.

★ ★ ★

Associated with every item is a concrete image or picture that will appear in your mind. A sharp, clear picture must be developed and shared with all the individuals working on this goal. This can be done through research. One of the best methods to do research is through shopping. The key is to bring the information home!

Methods to shop or research are:

1. Telephone – price comparisons.
2. Advertisements – direct mail flyers, magazine or newspaper ads.
3. Read Catalogs.

4. Visiting retail stores.
5. Discussing with neighbors and/or friends.
6. Reading consumer reports and magazines.
7. Searching the Internet.

An important step in research is to create a question-answer sheet. Before you start shopping, create a list of questions.

The following example - #4 Research Question and Answer Sample are basic guidelines. This list may grow as you reach each phase or step in the information-gathering process.

#4 Research Question And Answer Sample Sheet

1. Who is the best manufacturer?
2. Why are they the best?
3. If I buy this item right now, will it go up or down in value/price?
4. What guarantees or extended warranties come with the product?
5. What is the size, color? What are the other physical attributes?
6. Can this be purchased new? Used? Floor Model?
7. Are there any special features?
8. Where are all the local places I could purchase this item from?
9. Can I find it on the Internet cheaper?

As you begin to find the answers to your question, you will also obtain photos of your product. Attach the best picture of your goal to the container that holds the cash savings.

Keep your Question and Answer sheet and all other pieces of information you collect with your Goal List.

When it is time to buy, you may have to go back and re-ask some of the questions. This may be due to the amount of time that passed from the beginning to the end of the savings period. Even in a short period, such as three or six months, retail shops may have closed or new ones appeared. Some manufacturers of your product may have gone out of business or discontinued certain models. The price of your selected item may have gone up or down. You may also learn that prices are lower during certain months. You can save as much ast 10% to 50% on the retail price simply by knowing when to buy.

The more you learn about your goal item, the better informed you will be when you actually make the purchase. This makes for a better buying experience and you will be free to enjoy the product when you bring it home. You will not need to be concerned about the possibility that you have paid too much for an item, or that there are some unpleasant surprises.

ASSOCIATED COSTS

There are goals listed in #2 Example Goal Organization that are one-time purchases. But they will have ASSOCIATED COSTS that MUST be considered. The items are:

1. The personal computer
2. The used car

EXAMPLES - Purchasing the Personal Computer

The personal computer, by itself, may be a one-time purchase, but with it come many other expenses and new goals to consider. Bringing home a personal computer is one thing, but what do you want it to do? In order to use it, you will need to buy software. In order for the software to perform properly, it may require additional components, other pieces of hardware, such as: a printer, compact disk player, sound card, monitor, modem, joystick, keyboard, mouse, etc. There are many pieces, possibilities and potential upgrades.

And there is more. What about classes to learn to use the computer? Or self-instruction manuals and workbooks? What about a phone line or access to the Internet via Wi Fi?

Purchasing a personal computer requires a great deal of self-teaching. This is considered a highly complex purchase. Luckily, there are books written on "How to Purchase a Computer." They are in the local public libraries and available for purchase at book stores. Also, try-before-you-buy! Friends, public schools and the local public libraries will more likely have computers and a place to try them out. Always ask lots of questions.

A computer can be outdated within six month to one year. This is due to how quickly the product improvements and developments are being brought to the market. Timing is very important with this type of purchase. Finding someone you can trust to help you with this decision and the proper timing will save you money and disappointment.

If you wait long enough you many not even have
To buy a computer. The technology is changing
In a direction that will allow your television to be
Your access to the internet.

After making the one-time expense decisions for:

1. The personal computer
2. Hardware components and
3. Software packages,

there will be more decisions to make.

Will you want to access the Internet? This will be an entirely new are for you to research. This WILL NOT be a onetime expense. It will be a recurring, monthly expense.

1. There will be a one-time phone-line installation and/or connection fee.
2. A telephone monthly access charge.
3. A possible connect fee with and Internet Service Provider (ISP)
4. A monthly ISP service charge for access.

This entire process will need a new set of Questions and Answers to be researched for a new set of decisions. This should be done separately from the actual computer purchase, because you are going to need the time to make the best possible decisions. Since the personal computer is so versatile, there will be further enhancements desired in the future. Each enhancement may be a new goal. Each new goal will need to be researched before purchase.

Purchasing The New or Used Vehicle

Automobile purchasing, like purchasing a personal computer, is highly complex. The cost is very high. There is a great deal to consider. Some examples for your consideration are:

1. The automobile – New or Used
2. Type of automobile – Make, Model, Year.
3. Methods of purchase – Cash, Lease, Loan.
4. Responsibilities to assume – Registration, License, Tax and Insurance.
5. More Responsibilities – Maintenance, Upkeep and Repairs.

This is one of the most difficult items to purchase. But, the more time you invest in the research before purchasing your vehicle, the less money you will spend on the actual item. The more effort you put into understanding what you are paying for before you buy, the more pleasant your buying experience will be.

Asking and answering questions before you buy will help you stop impulse buying. The more expensive the item, the more research you will want to conduct. If you wish to own a new car, purchasing one at the first car lot you find may cost a great deal more than if you shopped. You need to know that you are getting what you paid for. Always consider if this deal is fair to you.

RESPONSIBILITIES ASSOCIATED WITH POSSESSIONS

With financial purchases comes responsibility. Each item needs to be researched carefully before any money is invested. When you work hard to save money to meet these goals, you want to make sure you are making the best possible decision when you buy. The idea is to make goals achievable and realistic.

The items you acquire represent the time and money you invested. Value what you have now and will acquire in the future. If you stockpile possessions, you may not have the time to enjoy them. Do not acquire more than you can care for. Take care of your possessions so they will last.

SLOW DOWN – THINK – DECIDE

After conducting your research, you will be ready to make purchases. You will need, however, to be mentally prepared to slow down, think and decide. You will need to slow down your actions. You will need to think about what you are doing. And finally, you will be prepared to make sound decisions. The following pages will serve as a reminder to you that there are many occasions where you can save money.

Is It Worth It?

Evaluation is a basic, fundamental step that is often overlooked when people deal with money. Decisions are made without planning. Begin the process of weighing out the pros and cons for each purchase. Allow yourself the time to think about what you are doing.

Slow Down! Society works at an accelerated pace. We rush to work, then we rush home. We rush to maintain our children, our home and our cars until everything is done at high speed. When we work and live at this speed, we can not take the time to think about the money leaving our hands.

Think! By slowing down the pace, it provides us with a chance to think about our actions. How many times have you been at the market and felt the push of the people behind you in line and noticed the pace of the rushed cashier? They are all in a hurry. You can easily be caught up in that feeling, because you also want to get out quickly. You waited in line. Your items are being checked out. The numbers flash on the screen so fast, you may not realize that you could be overcharged for some of the merchandise. Your brain is numb. You reach for cash and you overpay. You write a check and you forget to enter the important information in the check register. If only you had the time to think..!

Well... you do. When you are in line, think about and reexamine the items you are buying. Fill out the check, as much as possible, before you are in the front of the line. Record the information in the checkbook ledger and keep it open and available. When it is your turn to be served by the cashier, slow your pace down and think about recording the cost of the merchandise in all of the appropriate locations. Always wait for your receipt.

Usually, by the time you get in the checkout line, all you are thinking about is getting the merchandise home. There is no good place to inventory your purchases and verify the accuracy of the charges in the market. If you take a bus, you might take a gamble and attempt to check it at the bus stop, if there is room on a bench for you to sit. And if it appears safe. If you have a car and don't live far from the market, you just take everything home. Once home, again you are in a hurry. But you <u>must slow down</u>. Pull out each item and check it off the receipt. It only takes a few minutes. At the very least, know that you have the items you paid for.

Decide! If you find you have been overcharged for an item or several items, you may have to decide if it is worth the time to go back, find someone to provide you with service, and get back the money (or product) that is due you. Often, the amount may be so small, you decide against going back. You time may be worth more than a few pennies. But, if you find that $2.00 or $20.00 is due you, think again. Not only should this discrepancy be brought to the attention of the market, but you should make the effort to get back what was taken from you – your money.

There are many tasks we perform without thinking because we are in a hurry. Often, after the fact, we find that there is a penalty for running at this accelerated pace. In day-to-day living, it is important to enjoy the present. By slowing down the pace, for a few moments, before acting, you will benefit by having more control over the situation.

Research for developing questions and Finding answers is an important exercise.

To Complete This Chapter:

1.   Fill out Form 102 – Research Question and Answer Form.
2.   As you develop additional questions, write them down. You can use either a separate sheet of paper or the back of the form.
3.   As needed, use the phone to call local stores and ask questions about the product you are trying to learn about.
4.   Go to several stores to look at the product. If there are floor models available, try out the product.

RESEARCH SUMMARY

Every product or service is unique and will require their own set of questions that should be answered. Use the information collected as reference when selecting a product for purchase. After purchase, keep the information on file. The more complex the purchase, the more likely you will need to refer to this information again.

In order to achieve your goals and begin your research, you need to know where you are, financially. The following chapter – **Chapter 4 – Assessment –** will teach you how to determine your starting point. In other words, how much money you have today. Prepared with that knowledge, you will be able to make important and necessary financial decisions.

CHAPTER 4

Assessment

This chapter will teach you how to assess your current financial situation. It will guide you through the process needed to determine where you are now, financially. You will learn to document your income and payments due. The information you provide will be used to develop a current and future budget. You will decide how much cash you need to live on each week. The goals you established in Chapter 1 can realistically be achieved when you know where to start.

Study 3

The Lopez family always seemed to have money, but they were in trouble. Joe Lopez worked and made a good income. His wife, Marie stayed home to raise their two children. They owned a beautiful home, had two cars and provided their daughters activities after school. But, they lived in fear of the bills arriving, and not having enough to pay them.

They had never performed an assessment of their income and the money going out. When questioned, they remarked that they were afraid. Afraid? What did they fear? Isn't it more frightening to see the bills stack up and not pay them?

The assessment process was forcing them to face their fear. They were embarrassed about their past spending habits, and did not want to be reminded of them. Yet, without learning from the past, they could not build a better future. They were also afraid of having to modify their spending behavior to such an extreme, that they would have to live on much less. How would they know unless they could look at the situation as a whole?

Once Joe and Marie were ready to face their fear and create their first assessment, they realized they had many choices available to them. They did not have to go without food or clothing to pay off the bills. But, they had to make some adjustments in their spending habits. They needed to accomplish several steps in order to move forward.

First, they had to get organized. They had developed a lifestyle where, whatever was needed or wanted, the family would purchase the item(s) using credit cards without thinking of the consequences. They had to organize their wants and needs by writing down their goals and organize them by priority. Second, they had to learn to save for the things they wanted, instead of buying them the instant they desired. Third, they needed to develop a method to maintain their records. They had never organized their paperwork before, so this took about twenty-four weekend hours.

Once the tasks were completed, Joe and Marie were no longer afraid to look at their current situation and were eager to start their loan payoff and savings plans. This exercise gave them the first access to control over their finances.

WHERE ARE YOU TODAY?

Assessing your current financial position can be the most difficult step in the entire process of managing your money. Many people enter this process feeling highly emotional and it can cause anxiety, fear, concern, and even anger. At this point, you need to look at how much money, exactly, is coming in and going out. Simply put aside the negative emotions and look at where you are today. In the future, these emotions can be replaced with excitement. After assessing your current finances, **you will begin to save!**

Tools

Start with the following:

T   Pen
T   Pencil
T   Paper
T   Calendar
T   Calculator

Income

Mark the calendar with each day you expect a paycheck, in pencil. Enter your NET INCOME (which is the actual amount you expect to receive after taxes). The reason for entering this in pencil is that there is always a possibility that this amount could change due to a raise, a change in jobs, a change in tax rates or deductions. Mark this information from the current month, all the way through to December. You will need to obtain a calendar for next year so you can plan for one entire year's worth of income.

Holidays, Anniversaries, Birthdays

Continue marking the calendar. Mark all special events for which you will need to buy gifts of greeting cards. Each year there will be birthdays, anniversaries or holidays for which you would like to purchase something special for the people you care about.

Monthly Bills

Next, write on the calendar, each month, the bills you expect to arrive, and when the arrive. Rent or mortgage might be due on the first day of each month, but you may receive the bill on the 20th day of the previous month. Put (1) the name of the company or person you owe and (2) the amount on the day you EXPECT to receive the bill. Continue with all regular, monthly bills, such as the telephone company, gas, electric, water, etc.

Begin to change your concept of the BILL DUE DATE to: THEY ARE DUE WHEN THEY ARRIVE. The longer you hold on to a bill, the more chance you have of losing it or completely forgetting to pay it.

Irregular Bills

Think through this step carefully. If you have any bills that come less frequently than once a month, it is very important you also include these. For example, auto insurance may be due every 4 months or home insurance, once a year. Also consider donations to organizations or sending money to relatives. Do the best that you can to fill the calendar as completely as possible with anything irregular or less frequent than once a month.

#5 Calendar Example:

MARCH 2001

Sun	Mon	Tues	Wed	Thu	Fri	Sat
				1 Payday $610.67	2	3
4	5	6	7	8	9	10
11	12 Phone Co.: $37.00	13	14	15 Payday $610.67	16 Wtr & Pwr $65.00	17 Gas Co. $25.00
18	19 Credit Card $25.00	20	21	22	23	24
25 Anniversary	26	27	28 Rent $510.00	29	30	31

DETERMINE YOUR ALLOWANCE

How much cash do you need each week? Your allowance is the cash needed for day-to-day living expenses. Cash should not be used to obtain items such as gifts or spontaneous purchases. When you document how the cash is used, in advance, you have eliminated the guessing about where it has gone. The goal, in determining your allowance, is

to understand where the cash goes and control impulse buying.

#6 Weekly Allowance Determination Questions

T   Do you drive a car or take a bus? How much do you spend traveling to work and elsewhere?

T   Do you buy or pack a lunch? How often?

T   Clothing - Do you use a Laundromat or Dry Cleaner? How often?

T   Dinners - How often do you eat out?

T   Grocery or Convenience Store - How much do you spend? How often do you go?

T   The Little Things - Chewing gum, candy, cigarettes, soda, postage stamps, etc.

Cash is the money that slips easily through everyone's fingers. Until you can actually determine what you spend, you may continue to allow this to happen. Give yourself an honest figure to work with, then use this as your cash budget.

Each week, you will allow yourself a certain amount of cash for those items and no more. If there are price increases, however, you will need to adjust your allowance upward. The key is: know in advance the actual amount of money you need to live on for the week.

#7 Weekly Allowance Determination Example

Cash needed for One Week

Description	Amount
Transportation: Gas/Bus	$100.00
Clothes: Laundromat/Dry Cleaner/Soap, Bleach, Spot Remover	$20.00
Food: Breakfast	
..........Lunch	$60.00
...........Dinner	
...........Beverages/Snacks not included with meals	
Other:	
Other:	
Total	$180.00

Multiply by 4 or 5 weeks to get a monthly allowance expense. In our example, we will use $180.00.

$180.00 X 4 = $720.00
$180.00 X 5 = $900.00

We can average this out for the year.

There are 52 weeks in a year, so multiply:

$180 x 52 = $9360.00

This is the cash allowance required for the year based upon the figures used in this example form.

Now, divide by the 12 months:

$$\$9360 \ / \ 12 = \$780.00$$

This gives the average amount of cash required each month.

If the allowance of $780.00 is provided for a 4-week month, you will have money left over. If this allowance is provided for a 5-week month, you will most likely run a little short. It is best to work on a week-by-week basis.

When you have extra money left over at the end of the week, save it in one of the goal containers or in an emergency cash container. This can be anything such as a coffee can, a jewelry box, a peanut butter jar or a water bottle. Any type of container that will hold the cash and can be easily hidden within the household.

Use Form 104 - Allowance Determination Form and fill in the Amount Column as honestly as you can. Overestimate, if you need to. Three other lines have been added as "Other." If there is something you pay cash for, enter the description on this line and, again, provide an honest amount.

Although Grocery or Convenience Store has been added to this list, you should begin to pay by check any time you enter such an establishment. The reasons are:

1. Usually, this type of receipt is thrown away. For record-keeping purposes, it is better to write a check. Cash can quickly be used in these businesses. In later chapters there will be a discussion on using

and shopping for the best banks in order to start a checking account.

2. Often, products other than household foods are purchased at these establishments, such as lottery tickets, alcoholic beverages, cigarettes, paper products, business-related items, cosmetics, jewelry, gifts, postage, etc. Some of these items should be evaluated as luxury items, and others can be tax deductible.

To Complete This Chapter:

1. Obtain the tools listed in the beginning of this chapter.

2. Fill out:

    A. The Calendar
    B. Form 103 – Weekly Cash – Questionnaire Form
    C. Form 104 – Allowance Determination Form

3. Examine the information you wrote on the forms for any adjustments you can make to reduce the amount of cash you spend.

4. Estimate, as accurately as possible, the cash you need for each week. Overestimate if you believe you will run short.

5. Take any remaining cash, at the end of the week, and place it into one of your goal containers.

6. Start with a new cash allowance each week. This practice will develop into the habit of saving money.

ASSESSMENT SUMMARY

Filling out the calendar and determining an allowance are two basic, but very important steps in understanding your financial needs and spending. The reward for doing this work and following these guidelines carefully will be a major step towards saving cash. You are beginning to see where your money is going.

You will need the information you collected in this chapter in order to look at your financial situation more carefully in Chapter 5 – Maintaining Records. This will give you the chance to look at, not only your current spending, but also your future spending behavior. You will have the opportunity to save even more money.

CHAPTER 5

Maintaining Records

This chapter will teach you how to organize your information into monthly spreadsheets. The spreadsheets, when filled, will provide the instant "snapshots" of each month's income and expenses. By filling them out in advance, you create projections of future months. You will create a creditor contact list and begin to organize the paper that holds the vital information of past transactions. It is important to understand how much money you have and to be able to chart your progress. When this is accomplished, you will have the information required to make better decisions for the future.

It is important to maintain good financial records. The better you become, the more opportunities you will recognize and use to your advantage. Maintaining and keeping records requires effort and discipline. But the reward is, when you turn to your records, you will find exactly where you stand, financially. You will instantly know how far you have progressed in getting out of debt. You will know how close you are to achieving your goals. As a result, you will have access to your financial information WHEN YOU NEED IT.

Study 4

Karen worked full-time and had one small child. She had begun to handle the financial affairs of her household for only one year. In that time, she lost track of the bills she had and had not paid. Her dining room, living room and den had stacks of papers, envelopes, advertisements, file folders and boxes. She couldn't pay her income tax on time, because her paperwork was in such a mess. She felt that the situation was hopeless.

After reading Chapter 5 and soliciting the help of a good friend, she learned that there was a way to get clear of the problem. She asked her friend to watch her child while she got down to business. First, she studied #8 - Record Keeping Example and modified it to suit her style.

Before she could enter her information, she had to organize the paperwork. Her friend assisted her in the process, which helped keep the frustration level to a minimum. It took three solid weekends before she had the form design she liked and her pertinent information entered. But, once completed, she had everything she needed to get her income tax processed. She could also find the information required to determine which bills had been paid or not.

Karen did not want to end up in the same situation, again. So, she took it a step further. She created temporary holding places, all in one room. When she picked up the mail, it would go to the in-box. After opening, she would pay bills immediately, and put all other material in a decision-making-box. The bills and banking information were held in a "to be filed" box to be cleaned monthly. She would go through the decision-making box once a week and create a list of "to-do's" with a deadline for each.

Once the information was on the list, she tossed that material. She developed a system that was manageable for her to maintain regularly.

KEEPING RECORDS

Organizing the information from the calendar and then recording on a spreadsheet will quickly get you up to date. You will learn how much money comes in, where it goes out and where to plan for future unexpected expenses. To start, you will not need anything more fancy than a spiral-bound notebook.

Begin with twelve sheets, one for each month of the year. Start with the current month and write the month and year on the top of each page. Use your calendar as a guide. On the left side of each sheet, list all the companies and individuals names you will need to send payments to on a regular or irregular basis. In pencil, write down what you expect to pay for each bill.

IMPORTANT: The once-a-year expense or irregular bill should be included in each of the 12 months. For example, you may pay the electric bill every other month and the auto insurance once a year. Average an amount you expect to pay per year, then divide by 12 and enter it for all the months.

When you begin to pay the bills, write next to the penciled, estiamated amount, how the bill was paid. Enter the type of payment: cash, check, money order, cashier's check or credit card. Enter check numbers, where applicable.

On top of the penciled amount, enter the true amount that was actually paid, in ink. Once paid, check it off. In the last column, write the date that the bill was paid.

Net Income Total

In the upper right, total the amount you expect to receive for the month, again using your figures from the calendar. Use pencil, because wages, salary, income, etc. may change and our hope is for increases. #8 The Record Keeping Example shows that we expect to receive $1200.00 net for the month.

Allowance Total

What is your allowance for the month? Subtract this figure from the total amount you will be paid for the month. The example shows an allowance of $400.00. After subtracting this figure, we are left with $800.00. This is what we have to apply to our bills for the entire month.

Total Bills

Next, add all the bills for the month you expect to pay. This total includes all the payments, in the Amount Column. In our example, we used the amount of $743.87.

Is there anything left over?

Subtract the Total Bills from the amount we have left to pay for those bills.

The example shows:

$800.00 – $743.87 = $56.03 is remaining.

This example does not give us much room for emergencies or special occasions. We will work on this later.

1. Continue preparing the worksheets for each of the next twelve months. Total how much money you will expect to pay.
2. Below your Net Income Total, subtract the Total Bills to pay and look at your result.
3. From the result, subtract what you decided you need as an allowance for the 4 or 5 weeks of the month.

In this example, there is plenty of room to reduce the weekly allowance. We determined in the previous chapter that an allowance of $180.00 per week would be the minimum. We figured on $100.00 per week in the Record Keeping Example. We can compromise by bringing it to $100.00 per week.

Allowance at

$100.00 per week	
1200.00	Net Income total (per month)
– 400.00	Minus Allowance Total (per month)
800.00	
–743.97	Total Bills (per month)
56.03	Remaining for Emergencies

#8 Record Keeping Example

<u>January, 2001</u>

Net Income Total:	$1200.00
Minus (-) Allowance Total:	$ 400.00
Remaining to Pay Bills:	$ 800.00

Description	Amount	Paid	Form of Payment	Check Number	Date
Rent/Mortgage	$500.00	X	Check	1013	01/02/01
Telephone Company	$30.00	X	Check	1016	01/06/01
Gas Company	$26.75	X	Check	1017	01/02/01
Electric Company	$152.65	X	Check	1021	01/16/01
Water Company	$22.45	X	Check	1022	1/16/01
Trash Pickup	$12.12	X	Check	1023	1/16/01
Crunchy Credit Card Co.	0				
Best Bank Auto Loan	0				
Hobby Store	0				
Barber/Beauty Shop					
Vacation					
Gifts					

Total Bills:	$743.97
Emergencies:	$56.03

Additional Possible Monthly Expenses to Work from may include:

Postage
Dental
Medical

Pest Control

Dues/Fees (Association)

Basic Clothing

Entertainment – Cable/Satellite, Movies, Concerts, Dinners Out

Insurance – Auto, Life, Home, Apartment/Rental, Business, Medical, Dental

Home Services – Landscaper/Gardener, Housekeeper/Cleaning, Babysitting/Childcare, Eldercare

Credit Cards or Loans

Luxury – Personal Computer, Software, Peripherals, Supplies, Cellular Phone/Pager, Jewelry, Special/Luxury Clothing, Electronic Equipment, Hobby Equipment/Supplies (sports, music, art)

Home Business/Home Office Supplies

Vacation/Travel

Continuing Eduction – Tuition, Books, Supplies, Private Lessons/Tutoring, Field Trips/Travel, Lectures/Meetings, Seminars, Audio/Video Tapes, Specialized Courses

ASSESSMENT CHECK LIST

Is there any money left over? If you are in the negative, or close to zero, there are few options. You need to take action **now.** Look at your possibilities.

Your rent or mortgage may be too high for your income. You many need to move, sell your home or consider a roommate.

T   Are there any bills listed that can be reduced? For example, if the telephone bill is high, make a plan to change carriers.

T   Be more conservative with water, electric power and gas usage

T   If there are credit card debts or loans, can you pay minimum payments for now?

T   Are you too generous with your cash allowance? Can you cut back?

$ Can you increase your monthly income by:

1.   Getting a temporary, part-time second job.

2.   Selling some of your possessions through a garage sale or on EBAY

3.   Asking your employer for a raise.

4.   Getting additional family members to start working by using some of their special talents or skills.

5.   Starting a small, part-time home business?

The goal is to adjust monthly bills downward, or the monthly income upward, so that there is breathing room.

If you have a family, include everyone in the discussion of cutting back. With children that are school-aged, show them the math so they can also understand. Have each individual come up with an idea and discuss how these ideas will be implemented. It doesn't have to be tight forever, but let them know you will show them how much their ideas have saved the household the following month. The rewards will benefit everyone. The stress will be reduced, and the entire household can begin to focus better on achieving their goals.

Anyone who uses household money must be involved in learning and understanding how the money comes in and how much goes out. With this understanding comes a greater sense of responsibility. You will be pleasantly surprised how much your family members will want to help. Yes, even the children.

TAKE CONTROL BY KNOWING WHO YOU OWE

The next step is to organize every company or person you will be paying in the upcoming months. Create a list of every company and person you owe money to:

1. Full Name
2. Address where the bill should be sent
3. Phone number
4. Account number
5. Credit Card or Loan – Include the total payment due.
6. Your contact list will change with time, so date it at the top.

#9 Contact List Example

This contact list was created on Feb. 5, 2001.

Name	Address	Phone Number	Account Number	Balance Due
Landlord Name	1212 Ocean Ave., Los Angeles, CA 90020	212-555-1212	None - Rent	Monthly Only
Telephone Co.	1605 Phone Lane Los Angeles, CA 90020	212-555-1616	000-888-6256	Monthly Only
Gas Co.	4363 Gas Road Los Angeles, CA 90020	212-555-2424	GR04-353-0001212	Monthly Only

Electric Co.	2645 Electric Ave. Los Angeles, CA 90020	212-555-0101	ELEv56-8000121	Monthly Only
Water/ Trash Co.	11112 Water Way Los Angeles, CA 90020	212-555-1542	WT3207457891234	Monthly Only
Crunch Credit Card	45 Gateway Rd. Los Angeles, CA 90020	212-555-1050	CrCrC0516712	$1,141.00
Auto Loan 1	11 Alabaster Place Los Angeles, CA 90020	212-555-1200	Auto121-345-121	$12,144.00

MANAGING FINANCIAL PAPERWORK

There are not many people in the work that really enjoy filing and maintaining personal records. With all of the bills and "junk" mail we get, there is a lot of paper to deal with at the end of each month. It is overwhelming, time-consuming and tedious to keep up. If we don't maintain it, however, that essential piece we need can never be found.

Contained in many homes are the famous "junk files," the "junk drawers," the "junk boxes," and yes, even "junk rooms." Each essentially functions the same way. They all hold wads and wads of paper that no one has the time to manage or get to. Every time you look at it, it reminds you that your financial life is out of control.

This method of record keeping does not work very well. Especially when you need to find a receipt or document quickly. For example, you may have a tax audit and the IRS says you owe them money. You might have an insurance claim and show proof of ownership. Or you might have a dispute with a creditor and need to prove you are right.

Unless you can find the documents that prove your case, you will lose money.

YOU MUST GET THIS PAPER UNDER CONTROL!

There are several approaches:

1. Organize and file by Month.
2. Organize and file by Type of Expense.
3. Organize and file by Company Name.
4. Ask friends and family for help.

You can use file folders or large freezer-style bags to hold your paper collections. Walking through a stationary store or browsing online will show you a wide variety of products that are made available to make your life easier. This will give you lots of ideas, but you will need to decide on one method. Once you have decided on the supplies you like, stay with that style. **DO NOT CHANGE** from style-to-style. It can cost a great deal more if you do.

The easiest place to start is by sorting the paper into two piles.

1. Papers to dump in the trash, and
2. Papers to keep in a file.

After determining what needs to be kept, you need to decide on a filing method.

$ Month-to-Month - If you have very few expenses this is the easiest approach.

$ Type of Expense – If you are starting a home business you can use the RECORD KEEPING EXAMPLE descriptions as a guide to building your files. For example, you could organize the headings such as: RENT/MORTGAGE, TELEPHONE, GAS, ELECTRIC, WATER, etc. in alphabetical order. Each heading belongs to a separate folder. Then file the bills under that heading, chronologically – in date order, with the most current date in front.

$ Company Name – You may be able to access your files easiest by using the name of the company with which you have established an account. Each company belongs in a separate folder.

$ If you are overwhelmed with indecision and cannot get the motivation to start, ask your family and/or friends for help. You should see how other people organize their home files so you can DECIDE what works best for you. It is important that you set up a system, ANY SYSTEM and maintain it. You need to develop good habits to keep and access your most important documents.

The time you invest in organizing and maintaining the paperwork is money in your pocket. This will give you the power to control your money flow. You will have the ability to assess and reassess your situation in very realistic terms. You will know what you have spent, how much you earn, and how much you will need in the future. These records will tell you everything you need to know about your spending habits. Without organized records, you are only guessing.

Keep it simple. Stay with one method. The more practiced you become at filing and maintaining your records, the better you will become at retrieving them when they are needed.

Pay your bills near the area that holds your records. This keeps you near the information if you need to retrieve or refer to it. Also, when you have finished paying bills, it is more convenient to file them where they should go.

To complete this chapter:

1. Get the Calendar and Allowance Determination Form, which were completed in Chapter 4 and use the information for reference.
2. You will need the listed information to fill out the Monthly Expense Record Keeping Form.
3. When the first form has been completed, continue to build your projections by filling out copies of this form for the next eleven months.
4. Collect the contact information and fill out Contact List-Monthly Bills.
5. Decide how to organize your files and establish a weekly or monthly routine to maintain them.

RECORDS SUMMARY

You have learned that writing down your income and expenses are important in gaining an understanding of where you are, financially. You have written out your Net Income, your Allowance and the cost of your Monthly Bills on paper. By accomplishing this, you can determine very quickly whether you are living within your means, or if you need to take action to cut back spending.

You have also learned the importance of maintaining a contact list of who you owe. This has given you the ability to take charge of your payments. And finally, you have learned that keeping paper is not enough. You need to keep your documents organized. This has given you greater control over the unexpected financial situations that do arise.

Upon completion of this work, you will have the information that provides you with a current budget, projections for the next year and a contact list. The time and work invested to create this information will begin to pay off when you can review all of your income and payment activity. You will need the information collected in this chapter in order to begin **Chapter 6 – Cut Back Spending.** You will be able to see how your money is spent and begin to make good decisions to adjust income or spending as needed.

CHAPTER 6

Cut Back Spending

This chapter will teach you the basic process to aid you in cutting back your current expenses. A few examples are provided to emphasis and illustrate certain points. There is always a way to cut back, but the question is, do you really want to? This is the appropriate time to review your written goals and decide if your current spending habits are keeping you from achieving them.

RENT OR MORTGAGE

The cost of housing always seems to be high. For most people, this is the monthly expense that costs the most. Examine your monthly net income. Ideally, your rent or mortgage should be only one- quarter ($1/4^{th}$) of your net income. Depending on the city or the part of the country you live in, you may have to go as high as one-third ($1/3^{rd}$) this amount. But, never spend more than this. It can cost you more if you do not have enough to cover emergencies or repairs.

To figure your comfortable range for the monthly housing expense, calculate the following

EXAMPLE with Net Income = $1,500.00

$1,500 / 4 = $375.00 $1,500 / 3 = $500.00
$375 is 1/4th of $1,500.00 $500.00 is 1/3rd of $1,500.00

The example range from $375.00 to $500.00 is a safety zone to search in. If you go thigher than this, you will be adding to your anxiety every month until you can either:

1. Increase your monthly earnings
2. Cut other monthly expenses, or
3. Find another place to live that is within your comfort range.

This is the one bill that has priority over all of your other monthly costs. There is nothing more important that having a place to live and a guarantee that it will be there tomorrow. The best guarantee is to always pay this bill on time. Even if other bills are very late, this is the one you cannot play around with.

HEALTHCARE

Healthcare is the second priority. It has become a law and it is very expensive. I currently pay over $900.00 per month for Blue Shield Silver. But, you can get help to get that down based upon your income. In California, we have access to Covered California and Covered LA. Their web address is: www.coveredca.com. Please contact them for assistance.

GIFTS

Gift buying is a big part of peoples lives. The best way to begin controlling gift purchases is to start with a plan. Use the information you previously recorded on your calendar and write down each annual gift you expect to give for one year. You can begin to assess the quantity of individuals and the frequency of gift giving for each individual. List everyone and every occasion. Do not overlook anyone.

Examples:

- $ Birthdays
- $ Holidays
- $ Anniversaries
- $ Graduations

There are also many forms and aspects to gift giving. A gift is often more than the object itself. There may be the gift of food either purchased as a beautiful package, or food that you prepared. You might also give flowers or gift certificates, cash or checks. Other costs associated with gifts are wrapping paper, greeting cards, ribbons and bows, decorative gift bags or tissue paper.

This information should already be written on you calender. This will sever several purposes. First, you will not forget the events or individuals you wish to buy for. Second, you will be more prepared with a thoughtful and appropriate gift. Third, you will avoid impulse buying by making appropriate decisions before entering a mall or store.

Consider shopping at Goodwill or the Salvation Army. As for the bows, bags and cards, you can find these at the 99 Cent store at a fraction of the price of Target, Walmart and the rest.

Watch for Gift-Giving Pitfalls

Use checks whenever you purchase gift items. This will give you a record for filling out next year's form. It will also show you all the components, parts and pieces, large and small for expenses incurred with gift-giving.

Keep within your allowance budget by not using the cash. Your cash allowance is to live on week-to-week and your cash savings are for future emergencies. Gifts are not emergencies.

Shop for gifts on your day off from work and when you are not rushed. When you think about the people you care about most, you may have a tendency to overspend due to the good feelings you have about them. Another possible reason would be that you are trying to pay back for a previous gift that you may have recently received. Use good judgement.

Do not be ruled by your feelings when inside of the shopping establishment. Before entering, you should have already determined the gift you wish to purchase and how much you can afford. If you show people you live that you care about them through your daily actions, you will not need to try to compensate with an overly expensive gift on special occasions.

Save money by using the Gift Form as your gift budget and follow it.

RECYCLE YOUR MONEY

Cutting back on the amount of waste added to the environment is a serious issue. There is an added benefit as you become more ecologically aware.
Through cutting back and recycling, you save money. Immediate and lasting savings result by modifying bad habits and replacing them with good ones. Below is a sample of possibilities:

1. Cut back on the amount of water used each day. Some easy ways to accomplish this are:

    A. Stop the tap from flowing when brushing your teeth. Use a glass of water to moisten the toothbrush.
    B. Take baths instead of showers.
    C. Flush once when using the toilet.

2. Soaps and detergents are costly. Be aware of your current usage and cut back in tiny increments until

you find the proper amount that will still get the job done with:

A. Cleaning Laundry
B. Cleaning Dishes
C. Washing the Car
D. Washing Yourself

3. Start using ammonia, bleach, hydrogen peroxide, baking soda and vinegar for your cleaning needs to replace some of the name brand detergents and cleaners.

4. Reduce paper towel consumption by using rags whenever you can.

5. Reduce writing paper consumption by using the back of the page, too.

6. You may be eligible for tax deductions if you donate:

A. Appliances such as stoves, refrigerators, toasters, microwaves, computers and their parts, etc.
B. Clothes, shoes, towels, blankets, etc.
C. Household items, such as dishes, glasses, flatware, etc.

7. Repair the items you own, instead of buying new.

8. Buy used, instead of new.

9. Eat out less often. Prepare meals from home in advance.

There are many ways you can cut back on regular household expenditures if you take the time to consider alternatives and become aware of the options available. There are also ways to reduce unexpected expenditures if you think about your actions in a variety of settings.

The following section provides a few examples illustrating why you need to take the time to think about your actions.

EVALUATE YOUR ACTIONS IN DOLLARS AND CENTS – BY USING COMMON SENSE

Example 1:

Have you ever tossed a piece of paper on the sidewalk or thrown trash out of your moving vehicle? Before you do these things, you might begin by asking yourself if it is worth it. If you get caught performing these actions by the police, you know you will receive a ticket and will be required to pay a fine. Is it worth paying $100.00, $500.00 or $1,000.00 for the privilege of littering? Some people may think so. But, to individuals that could use that amount of money to pay rent, buy groceries or purchase winter clothing, this may not be the case.

Example 2:

Have you ever been influenced by peer pressure? Imagine that it is Friday afternoon, and just before quitting time, someone shouts, "Let's meet at the bar down the street for a beer!" It sounds agreeable to the group. After work, everyone meets and begins to talk and drink. No one wants to be the first to get up and walk out. So, the first hour passes. Then the second. And in that time the bar tab has gone up very fast. When do you pay your share and go home?

Example 3:

Have you ever made a mistake with someone and tried to compensate by giving a gift? This is done frequently with lovers or spouses, or among individuals at work. Mistakes happen. If you hurt someone's feelings or cause a problem, take care of it directly and immediately. Giving gifts may be interpreted as insincere and does not fix the problem. Try not to be influenced to part with your money out of guilt.

Understand where the money goes. Understand why. When you learn about your motives, you will make better decisions about where you would really like to put your money.

To complete this chapter:

1. Fill out the Gift Form for the end of this year and into the next.
2. Determine an estimated amount you will spend for each individual item.
3. Add this information to the 12 Monthly Expense Record Keeping Forms.

You will have a more accurate account of the actual money you expect to spend in the coming year.

SPENDING SUMMARY

You have learned to think about your actions and motives before you spend. You have examined your listed expenses as a potential area to reduce costs. The daily, weekly, and monthly expenses, such as housing, phone, healthcare, postage and utilities will cost you less as you adjust bad habits and replace them with good ones.

No one can do it all alone. After completing this chapter, you are ready to begin Chapter 7 - Family - Get Everyone Involved. You will learn that you can easily share what you have learned about saving money. Cutting back on spending will be easier as you involve everyone in the household.

CHAPTER 7

Family - Get Everyone Involved

This chapter will teach you how to teach others about money. Whether you currently live alone, or have a family, you will want to teach those individuals you care about how to handle money. Typically, one person is responsible for preparing and paying bills. It it important that everyone becomes and remains aware of their money matters. Many relationships may end up in complete and final separation or divorce due to one individual maintaining total control. In sharing this responsibiity, you will be sharing the decision-making role. This will help you avoid mistakes.

★   ★   ★

Study 5

Maria could not understand how people were able to put money into their savings every month. She worked as an executive secretary and made a good income. But, she did not have a savings account established. After learning about starting small, she said, "I always thought that $5.00 would be too small to start a savings plan!" She learned that there is no amount that determines where the savings plan should start. It was a matter of organization and putting a plan to work. Since then, she has saved enough to open a saving account and a CD (Certificate of Deposit) at her bank.

★   ★   ★

You never know what the future will bring. A disabling accident, an unforseen illness or death can bring financial devastation to your family. It can be worse if it happens to you and you are the only account holder and household money manager. Even if your spouse chooses not to learn or has complete trust in you, it is important that you explain why it is necessary for him/her to understand and practice handling money. This is a responsibility you must share, and it is even more critical if you have children.

As you begin to teach someone you love about household financial management, remember, money is an emotional subject. You must remain patient, calm and diplomatic. Especially if your spouse is not interested, but learning because they feel obligated.

Explain how to manage money by providing many small lessons over time. Don't try to teach too much in one session. Start with one concepts, such as how to operate the ATM and record the withdraw in your checking account ledger.

TEACH YOUR CHILDREN THROUGH PLAY

You can never begin to teach your children too early. There are many aspects to understand about money. The more practice you can give your children now, the fewer problems they will have as adults. And the fewer problems YOU will have as they become adults. You can create games to teach your children the denominations of cash and the value of money.

Example 1: You have a $1.00, $5.00, $10.00 and $20.00 bill. You child has a mountain of coins. As the child to pull out the correct amount of coins to equal each bill. This can be done with quarters, dimes, nickels and pennies. It can be more fun for the child to have a wallet or purse.

Example 2: When the child can play the game with confidence, you can create a competition with other children, or race against the clock to increase the challenge.

Example 3: Children love to use their imagination and often pretend that they are adults. Ask them to pretend that their bedroom is a store. Have them set it up, according to their imagination, i.e. using a box lid as a cash register, arranging their belongings for a store display, label their belongings with a price on non-permanent stickers. They could dress up as Mom or Dad, carrying a purse or wallet with money. Have them take turns shopping and buying items.

A great investment are some classic games found at toy stores, game shops and department stores. Some of these games are **Monopoly** or **The Game of Life.** Not only do they bring the family together, but the children continue to learn about money through play.

The next section discusses actual cash and coins. Children can also be helpful by organiztion money for a bank deposit.

CASH AND COINS - DENOMINATIONS

When to Count Pennies

Saving for what you want takes time and discipline. But, using the weekly loeft-over cash from allowances and other areas can be fun.

Rolling Coins – The table below is a simple guide. Sometimes bank tellers can have a difficult time counting coins because each type represents a different amount, and a different number of coins are required for filling rolls.

#12 Example Cash Counting Form

COINS	CASH VALUE	ROLL CASH VALUE	# OF COINS TO FILL A ROLL
Quarter	.25	$10.00	40
Dime	.10	$ 5.00	50
Nickel	.05	$ 2.00	40
Penny	.01	$ 1.00	50

You must write your account number on every wrapper in case of a miscount. Do this while the wrapper is flat, it is easier to do. Do not bring the wrappers to the bank without the account numbers, because the tellers will instruct you to do so before accepting them.

When coins are wrapped, you know exactly how much cash you have. So, after wrapping, do not keep too much of this cash in the home. The wrapped coins and paper money are too tempting to use and can easily be stolen. Evaluate the frequency you should be counting and taking this money to the bank. Remember, if you are adding one or five dollar bills to your cash savings, the total amount of cash can add up quickly.

INVOLVE EVERYONE SUMMARY

In this chapter you have learned to share what you know about money with our family. You will need to keep your instructions simple, clear and fun for everyone. As you begin to work on saving money, you will find your family will be your best support.

You have also learned that there is no amount of money that is too small to begin your savings plan. From pennies come rolls of pennies which grow to single dollar bills, to fives and tens. This small amount of cash accumulates quickly, especially when the entire household cooperates. You are now ready to begin Chapter 8 - U.S. Banks - in order to learn about the benefits of using a bank to keep your savings safe.

CHAPTER 8

U.S. Banks - What They Can Do For You

This chapter will teach you how to compare banks for the best services and prices. Three comparison examples are provided: (1) Banks as institutions, (2) Checking accounts and (3) Savings accounts. Requirements and minimums to open accounts are discussed. Comparison examples and a rating system are provided to assist in this process.

All banks offer many different types of accounts with various fees. Shopping for the right bank is as important as saving the money in the first place. You will want to keep your money in the bank or savings & loan you determined will provide you with the best service and lowest cost.

Banks, savings banks, savings & loans, thrifts, credit unions, and now brokerage firms are all businesses that provide services to assist you in handling your money. They are often referred to as institutions, but, like all businesses: THEY ARE IN THE BUSINESS TO MAKE MONEY. Banks charge a wide variety of fees for the various services they offer their customers. They provide short-term and long-term loans to individuals and businesses. The receive income from interest on loans, and providing services, such as handling the contracts and paperwork involved for loans.

It is important to have a bank account. It can accelerate your possible savings ten-fold. Your money is safe and insured up to $125,000.00. Your money can begin to work for you by earning interest. You will also benefit from the increased accuracy in your record keeping. You will find you have greater control over your income and monthly bill paying, and less money will leave your hands, than dealing on a cash-only basis.

One of the best examples of spending too much, when you have no bank account, is the check cashing business. Their fees, to accept your check and provide you with cash, are ridiculously high. Compare the cost of getting your own money through a check cashing business versus a bank. Using a bank, there is no fee to cash a check and your money is safe.

Each type of bank has a long list of services they can provide to the average consumer. Some are:

- $ Checking Accounts
- $ Savings Accounts
- $ Money Market Accounts
- $ Certificates of Deposit
- $ Safety Deposit Boxes
- $ Travelers Checks
- $ Money Orders

$ Cashier's Checks

$ Mortgage Loans

$ Business Loans

$ Personal Loans

$ Auto Loans

$ Credit Cards

$ Debit Cards

$ ATM or Automated Teller Machine Services

All banking services have a price. Your goal is to be able to access as many services you need for the lowest possible fees. You will need to comparison shop. The easiest way to do this is to use BankRate.com.

Your very best deal, if you qualify, is having an account through a credit union Usually, they are restricted to particular employers or employees. But, due to sweeping changes in business and industry, credit unions are expanding their fields of membership. To find out if you are eligible to join a credit union, contact the Credit Union National Association (CUNA), the public releations office at 800-358-5710.

REQUIREMENTS

To open a bank account, you are required to have two forms of identification.

1. The first piece of identification must have a photo of you on it. This can be an immigration card, driver's license, and state or student identification card.
2. You must also have a social security number.

This is required for two reasons: (1) For your protection, both for identity and financial purposes and (2) To have you pay the proper amount of tax on the income you will earn after keeping it in the bank.

MINIMUMS

Banks will state that they require a certain minimum amount of money that you do not touch while you use their checking, savings, money market accounts and CDs. You will want to use the bank that offers the lowest minimum requirement. If you can meet that minimum and maintain it always, you will be eligible for many free benefits. Every bank is different, so please check this carefully while you are comparing. If you cannot maintain the bank minimum, you will be charged every single month for the privilege of having an account at that bank. That can be very expensive.

To Complete This Chapter:

1. Find a bank to establish your checking and/or savings accounts.
2. Find several banks in your local area. Use BankRate.com
3. Compare the checking accounts.
4. Compare the savings accounts.
5. Select the best bank for you.

BANK SUMMARY

You have learned that banks are necessary to assist you in handling and managing your money. You have learned that you must carefully screen between banks and their services to select the one that will work best for you and your special financial needs. By comparing banks and their fees, you can save hundreds of dollars per year.

When you have completed this chapter, you will be ready to start Chapter 9, which will teach you how to save money through your checking account.

CHAPTER 9

Save Through Your Checking Account

This chapter will teach you how to save by using a checking account. You will learn the parts of a check and how to properly fill one out. You will learn how to fill out a deposit slip to add money to your account. You will learn to fill out a withdrawal slip to take money from the account. The end of this chapter provides the guidelines and precautions when using the ATM.

Study 6

Alan was a single father with one child. He lost his job and his wife left him in the same week. The bank accounts were cleaned out and he had only $10.00 in his pocket. He did not want to end upon the street, especially with a child. So, he sought out friends that would take him in until he could work out this set of circumstances.

Alan was determined not to let these series of events rule his life. He found employment in three days and began to be paid on a weekly b asis His income was barely over minimum wage. Due to his desperation of having nothing, Alan began to make some money mistakes. First, each check was cashed at a check cashing business, which took a percentage off the top of his earnings. Second, the money was being spent within two days. Third, there was nothing to live on for the rest of the week.

Alan wanted to rent an apartment by the end of one month. But, with this current spending behavior, his goal would not be achieved. So, Alan's money handling had to change.

First, he established one money container. Second, he opened a checking account. He learned to establish a cash emergency fund in the money container and an emergency buffer fund in the checking account. In one month, he saved the money for a deposit and moved into an apartment. In three months, he had $1,000.00 in a savings account by using the checking account buffer system of rounding up for each check written, and rounding down for each deposit. In six months, his empty apartment was nicely furnished. He had a natural talent for finding good deals when purchasing furniture and appliances. And his savings account continues to grow.

Alan is an exceptional example and it would be difficult to match the speed of his success. But, his desire to achieve his goals quickly was strong. His determination and motivation were to create a suitable home environment for his child.

★　★　★

#19 Example Checkbook Ledger

NUMBER	DATE	DESCRIPTION OF TRANSACTION	PAYMENT/DEBIT (-)		CODE*	FEE(-)	DEPOSIT/CREDIT (+)		$ 1686.00
1818	2/1	A Mortgage Bank Home Mortgage	$ 1348	27		$	$		-1350.00
									336.00
1819	2/1	Number One Gas Co.	36	12					-40.00
									296.00
1820	2/1	Al's Supermarket Groceries	121	32					-125.00
									171.00
ATM	2/1	Cash	100	00					-100.00
		Allowance for 2 weeks							71.00
Dep.	2/15	Company Paycheck Miguel					696	23	+690.00
									761.00
Dep.	2/16	Company Paycheck Miguel					122	16	+120.00
									881.00

One of the quickest methods to build your savings is by using your checking account. Every transaction is recorded in the checkbook ledger. Usually, several checks are written in a month. Each check amount should be written twice in the checkbook ledger if you are using two lines for each transaction. Us this style to begin recording your new checkbook savings.

#19 Example Checkbook Ledger shows numbers in the Payment and Deposit Columns. The numbers in these columns are copied into the Balance Column for subtraction or addition.

Notice that the EXACT numbers are placed in the Payment column, but not in the Balance Column.

> - The numbers are ROUNDED UP when copied to the BALANCE COLUMN from the PAYMENT COLUMN.

> - The numbers are ROUNDED DOWN when copied to the BALANCE COLUMN from the DEPOSIT COLUMN.

Each check written for payment or deposit is providing an opportunity for you to save.

PARTS OF THE CHECKBOOK LEDGER

Most checkbook ledgers are standard. Each column heading has special meaning:

1. USE BOTH LINES (the light and dark) for each transaction. Checkbook ledgers are provided free at the bank where you have an account. You will see the information better and you will develop a good habit of keeping better records and account buffers.

2. NUMBER COLUMN - Use this column to record the check number for identification. Use the same column to enter:

   - ATM cash withdrawals
   - DEP for Deposit
   - AUTO - For Automatic withdrawals for bill payments

3. DATE - Date of the transaction

4. DESCRIPTION OF TRANSACTION - Use the top line for the company or person name that the check is made out to. Use the bottom line to describe the purchased item or service.

5. PAYMENT/DEBIT (-) COLUMN - Enter the ACTUAL amount of the check or ATM withdrawal.

6. CODE - Some people use this column to determine if an item is tax deductible, by entering a checkmark in those that apply. You should consider using this column by marking the fact that the checkbook statement holds the same information that has been written on the check. Another application is to enter actual codes such as:

   - D = Deposit
   - DC = Debit Card
   - ATM = Automatic Teller Machine Transaction

- AP = Automatic Payment
- TT = Telephone Transfer (or Wire)
- T = Tax Deductible

7. Fee (-) Column - Applies to any bank charges, such as monthly or ATM fees.
8. Deposit/Credit (+) - Enter the ACTUAL amount of the money or paycheck being deposited.
9. BALANCE - The ROUNDED amounts of the Payment/Debit (-) Column or the Deposit/Credit (+) Column appear on the top line. The subtraction or addition provides the remaining balance that appears on the second line.

In #19 Example Checkbook Ledger, the first entry under PAYMENT/DEBT columns hold the exact check amount ($1,348.27). The second entry, in the same row, in the column labeled BALANCE holds a rounded up amount ($1,350.00). This shows a little bit more money is spent for each check written. By subtracting the rounded up amount, you are hiding the true balance.

The same is done for each deposit. The rounding up or down performed in this example is only done to the next $5.00 increment. To accelerate savings, rounding can be done in $10.00 increments as well. To slow down savings, round out to the next dollar. Don't count the pennies. It's like adding change from your pocket to your cash containers. This hidden savings is called a checking account buffer.

How much was saved in the example for a total of six transactions? It's easy to figure, just a little time consuming. In our example, we saved a total of $17.48.

Hold off determining your true account balance until your monthly checking account statement arrives. You will avoid the temptation of spending it. Let it grow so that you can have a good buffer established for the unforeseen problems and emergencies.

HOW TO WRITE A CHECK

Writing a check is simple. Identifying the parts of a check and understand what they mean is briefly described below.

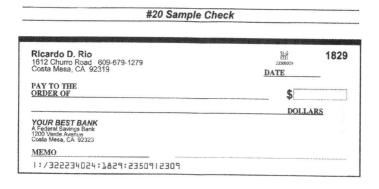

#20 Sample Check

Ricardo D. Rio
1612 Churro Road   609-679-1279
Costa Mesa, CA 92319

91-2
1221
23509309

1829

DATE

PAY TO THE
ORDER OF

$

DOLLARS

YOUR BEST BANK
A Federal Savings Bank
1200 Verde Avenue
Costa Mesa, CA 92323

MEMO

⑆322234024⑈1829⑆23509⑉2309

Your name and address will appear in the upper left corner of the check. It is optional to include your phone number. Most retail locations will ask for your phone number and enter it by hand if it does not appear on the face of the check. Also optional is to include your driver's license or state license identification number. Although having this information printed on your check can expedite your transactions at a check-out line, you may not want too much information included, in case your checkbook is ever stolen.

The proper number to use when filling out a deposit slip is located on the upper line after the "/" slash symbol. Our example shows "3222". This is called the BANK ROUTING NUMBER. The bank routing number identifies the bank where the funds are from. Using this number will help you trace your deposit, if there should ever be a problem.

The date is for the actual day you fill out the check. Pre-dating and Post-dating checks is considered unethical and illegal.

"Pay to the Order of" line should be filled out as fully as possible. Try to use the entire lne and DO NOT use abbreviations. If this check is stolen, it will make it more difficult to alter the check if you have written across the entire line.

The "$" box will contain the numerical symbols for the actual amount of the check. Often, this box will be filled with numbers as $16.32/100 for $16.32.

The line below will contain the amount completely written out in words.

"Sixteen Dollars and 32/100."

Below the amount shows your bank name and address. Sometimes the bank phone number is included.

The last line, "MEMO", is a small area for you to place a note to yourself that will better describe the transactions. For example, you may make a check out to Luis & Associates. The name does not indicate the type of business it is or the type of service or product you received. When you write a check, place in the "MEMO" line   TAX ACCOUNTING   for example.

It will help you to remember why you wrote this check when you are going through returned checks weeks later.

The line to the right of the "MEMO" line is where you write your signature. To avoid problems and/or complications, sign your check the way your name appears in the printed section.

IMPORTANT: Just because you have checks left in your checkbook does not mean you have money left in the bank!!

HOW TO MAKE A DEPOSIT AND WITHDRAW WHILE IN THE BANK

Filling out a deposit or withdraw slip may be the easiest lessons to learn. It is essential that you never forget to record these transactions in your account ledger. This is the step that is typically forgotten.

When to enter the transaction in your checkbook ledger:

- While at home – before going to the bank
- When filling out the deposit or withdrawal slip
- While waiting in line
- During the actual transaction
- At the moment the receipt is handed to you by the bank teller.

DO NOT wait until you leave the bank. It is too easy to forget.

How to Fill Out a Deposit Slip

Deposits consist of either cash or checks. When making deposits you must fill out the deposit slip completely. When depositing checks, you are required to enter the bank routing number next to the amount. The back of the deposit slip lists several lines for each individual check.

#21 Sample Deposit Slip

DEPOSIT **Best Bank**

Customer Name (Please print): | Date:

Form # (LM001)

Cash Received By: (Please sign in bank employee's presence)

IMPORTANT NOTICE   A HOLD FOR UNCOLLECTED FUNDS MAY BE PLACED ON FUNDS DEPOSITED BY CHECK OR SIMILAR INSTRUMENT. THIS COULD DELAY YOUR ABILITY TO WITHDRAW SUCH FUNDS. THE DELAY, IF ANY, WOULD NOT EXCEED THE PERIOD OR TIME PERMITTED BY LAW.

Account Number

Cash

Check Total from back side

Sub total

Less cash received

$

1:5011:0210:   30

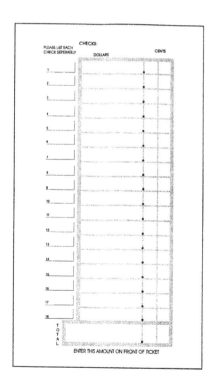

CHECKS:

PLEASE LIST EACH CHECK SEPERATELY

DOLLARS

CENTS

1
2
3
4
5
6
7
8
9
10
11
12
13
14
15
16
17
18

TOTAL

ENTER THIS AMOUNT ON FRONT OF TICKET

How to Fill Out a Withdrawal Slip

The withdrawal slip is far less complicated than the deposit slip. You are required to:

1. Fill in your name as it appears on the account.
2. Today's date
3. The account number from which you wish to withdraw from
4. The actual amount of money you wish to withdraw.

Whenever you remove money using a withdrawal or deposit slip, you will be required to sign it with a bank employee as a witness. This is a protective service for you and your account. Your signature may be matched to the signature card they have on file for verification.

The back of the withdrawal slip, identified by the light writing, is reserved for the bank employees to fill.

WITHDRAWAL

Best Bank

Customer Name (Please print): | Date:

Form # (LM002)

I (we) apply for withdrawal of the amount shown and acknowledge receipt of this sum.

X

(Please sign in bank employee's presence)

Account Number

Withdrawal Amount

$

1:5011:0210:

This area for office use only.

Driver's License #

Identikey #

Other I.D.

THE ATM - MONEY DOES NOT GROW ON TREES

ATM = Automated Teller Machine

The ATM has become one of the most convenient tools for banks and their customers. They can be found at most banks all over the world, as well as grocery stores and gas stations. This convenience comes at a price. The price can be quite literal, a charge or fee for using the system. The price can also be safety. Be aware of the cost when using an ATM.

Most Important - Be Safe

1. Always use the ATM in daylight
2. Always take someone with you.
3. Upon opening an account, take a healthy handful of ATM deposit envelopes and MAIL IN deposit envelopes with you. Both types of envelopes are different. The ATM deposit envelopes will required deposit information on the outside of the envelope. The MAIL IN deposit envelope will have the return address of the bank. This will give you the opportunity to fill out everything in the comfort and safety of your own home.

When Preparing a Deposit:

1. Have the check(s) signed.
2. Put your account number below the signature on the back of the check.
3. Write "For Deposit Only" whenever you need to carry a signed check.

4. Fill out your deposit slip and total the amount.
5. Enter transactions in your checking or savings account ledger.
6. If you are making a withdraw, enter this in the ledger before you leave the house.
7. Verify that you have both the ATM card and deposit envelope with you before you leave the house.

Protect Your Card

If your bank does not provide a "card sleeve" for protection, making one by cutting up an envelope is simple. There is nothing worse than not being able to access your money on a weekend due to the magnetic strip being demagnetized.

If you need a card to be reissued, some banks an take as many as five business days.

Protect Your Account

1. Never leave your receipts at the site of the ATM machine.
2. Protect your PIN (Personal Identification Number).
3. Record your PIN with your home financial records.

Protect Your Cash

After retrieving your cash from the ATM, fold it up small, to fit in the palm of your hand, or promptly slip it into your wallet. Do not leave the ATM until your cash is concealed and you have checked your belongings.

Protect Yourself

Always look at the entire situation, the neighborhood, the lights, the people, etc. before walking up to the ATM. Even though ATMs are monitored by a security camera, you must be responsible for your own safety.

Watch for ATM Service Charges

- You may be charged at a branch, but not at your home branch.
- You may be charged if you use the other bank's ATMs.
- You may be charged if you use the ATM to make a purchase at a convenience store or gas station.

To complete this chapter:

1. You must have a checking account.

   - By searching Bankrate.com, you have already determined the bank that serves you best.

- Now, you can use your next paycheck, or the saved cash in your containers, to start your checking account.
- Plan to spend enough time to have all of your questions answered by the New Accounts Representative.
- Take their business card, in case you have any other questions you need to ask later.
- Add them to your contacts.

2. After opening an account, ask for the following supplies:

   - An ample supply of deposit and withdrawal slips
   - Deposit-by-mail envelopes.
   - ATM envelopes
   - You will automatically be given a small amount of checks and a checkbook ledger to start.

3. Ask for an ATM card. Depending upon the bank you choose, you may not receive one that day. If could take up to a week to receive a new ATM card.

4. You are now ready to practice saving money through your buffer by using your checking account.

CHECKING ACCOUNT SUMMARY

In this chapter you have learned how to fill out checks, deposit and withdrawal slips. You have been introduced to the convenience of ATM service and to be cautious when using this service. You have learned to carefully document each transaction in the checkbook ledger. Start carefully and slowly to develop the good habits you will need. These good habits will reduce your chance of error and enhance your ability to save money.

CHAPTER 10

Balance Your Checkbook

This chapter will teach you how to balance the checkbook using the bank statement. Samples are given to illustrate how the checkbook statement will appear. The instructions discuss the many parts that make up the statement and how each section is figured to determine the balance. The buffer is figured in at the end of this chapter. This is your most important lesson.

#23 Sample Bank Statement (Front – Page 1)

Your Best Bank	Statement Period: 2/7/2001 to 3/7/2001
A Federal Savings Bank	Acct. No.: 123-456789101
1200 Verde Ave., Costa Mesa, CA 92323	Check Items Enclosed: 36
800-123-4567	Page Number 1
Richard D. Rio	
1612 Churro Road	
Costa Mesa, CA 92319	

Bank announcement of services and
products available to customers
Best Bank Checking Summary

Beginning Balance	Deposits	Withdrawals	Fees & Charges	Interest Credited	Ending Balance
1727.93	7567.04	6622.00	10.00	1.81	2664.78

CHECKS

Number	Date	$ Amount
1816	03/03	50.00
**1819	02/09	105.00
**1821	02/10	87.71
**1823	02/10	42.31
1824	02/24	50.00
1825	02/25	49.00
1826	02/25	49.00
1827	02/25	58.00
1828	02/24	32.55
1829	02/24	17.32
1830	02/24	97.60
1831	02/24	15.35

★=Break in Sequence   Total Checks Cleared: –5251.10

DEPOSITS

Date	Description	$ Amount
02/13	Automatic Deposit of Paycheck	$1567.27
02/21	Deposit ATM Costa Mesa #1	$2005.04

Total Deposits Shown: +3572.21

Easy Steps to Balance your Checkbook:

– Update your check register
    Add any interest; subtract any service charges
– Determine outstanding items
    List any items in your check register not checked off
– Balance Your account

1. Take all enclosed returned checks sent to you from the bank and arrange them in numerical order, using the check number in the upper right corner, lowest number to highest.

2. Check for numerical mistakes – Verify that the amount on the check matches exactly the amount on the statement. If not, circle the item on the statement. You will need to contact your bank if there is an error between the check amount and the recorded amount on the statement.

3. Checks – open your checkbook ledger. Match the first check number from the statement to the check number on the ledger. Verify that the amount on the statement matches exactly the TRUE AMOUNT written in the debit column in the check ledger. If not, correct the discrepancies in your ledger.

Important: Circle any listed check on the statement that you DID NOT enter in your check ledger. You will need to write the missed checks in your checkbook ledger and subtract them from your balance.

BALANCE YOUR LEDGER USING BUFFERS

Numerical Mistakes

If you have been using the two-line method in your checkbook ledger, you will have the actual check amount in the Debit column and the rounded up number in the Total or Balance column of the checkbook ledger. Check the accuracy of your Actual check amount in the checkbook ledger with the check amount on the bank statement. If the discrepancy amount is small (only pennies), simply fix the actual check amount in the debit column. If the discrepancy is large, write the amounts on the top of the checking account statement and circle the amounts.

1. Total your Discrepancies
2. Enter Any Checks, ATM Transactions, Withdrawals or Deposits from your Check Ledger That have not cleared.
3. Total the Outstanding Checks.
4. Total the Deposits not Shown.
5. Find the Ending Balance
6. Add Total Deposits not shown t the Ending Statement Balance.
7. Subtract total Checks and Withdrawals from the new Total.
8. Find your Checkbook Balance.

HOW TO CALCULATE THE BUFFER

Find your buffer amount. Subtract the checkbook balance from the current balance number found in step 7 above, from the statement.

The Total Buffer is the amount you saved!

How To Manage The Buffer

When your buffer is more than $500.00, transfer the difference into your savings account.

A quick summary of the transactions are:

Ending balance (from statement) $ _____

Add deposits not credited: + _____

Subtract Outstanding Checks   - _____

Total Current Balance: = _____

Make sure the checkbook balance is correct!

After determining your balance, you can determine your buffer amount:

Corrected Checkbook Balance $ _____

Subtract Balance in Checkbook: - _____

Total Buffer Amount: $ _____

UPDATE 2020: Bank of America has a "Keep the Change" Savings Program. Build your savings automatically. Round each purchase to the nearest dollar and turn spare change into savings. All you need to get started is a check account with a debit card and a savings account. What could be easier?

CHECKBOOK SUMMARY

Your checking account statement will arrive every month at approx. the same time. Be prepared to allocate at least one hour of quiet time to balance your checkbook. Collect all the tools you will need to proceed.

Use this chapter as a guide to assist you with balancing your checkbook each month. Start slowly and carefully. Once you have become practiced and proficient, you will be able to follow these steps quickly and efficiently. The reward for this work will be to discover the hidden savings contained in the buffer.

You are now ready to learn how to establish and manage Credit, which is covered in Chapter 11.

CHAPTER 11

Credit

This chapter will teach you an independent approach to establishing credit. Due to the burden that many Americans face by owing too much, following is a discussion of the importance of being debt free. This chapter provides guidelines for paying off all debts. Other topics include shopping for the best credit card rates, how to receive credit counseling and how to obtain free credit reports.

Study 7

Jerry was having a difficult time because he could not get a home improvement loan. The loan officer told him that he was "upside-down" in his loans. This meant that he owed more than they determined his home was worth and believed he would have a difficult time paying back his debt. He had a home mortgage, one personal loan and three credit cards outstanding. He had a very low interest rate for the home mortgage and personal loan, and he has been paying on them for fifteen and five years, respectively. The trouble was the credit cards.

He loaned his credit card to family members. He permitted a married couple to use one card, and the debt was $15,000.00. He permitted a niece to use the other card, and the debt was

$5,700.00. The card he used had a debt of $2,200.00. The card he used personally had an interest rate at 19%. There was also a cash advance in the amount of $500.00 due on his credit card. The interest rate was at 24%. Jerry needed a way out of his situation.

First, Jerry requested that the married couple and his niece begin accelerating their payments by adding additional principal to each payment. They had always paid the minimum on time, but his situation changed and his credit was not "at risk." Second, he collected all the advertisements for new credit cards he had received in a one-month period. Upon examining the cards closely, he discovered one that had an annual percentage rate of 5.9% for the term of six months, then it would increase to a fixed 14.9% APR.

He transferred his debt from the 19% credit card and from the cash advance at 24% to the low-interest 5.9% card. Even if he continued to make the same payment on the new card, as he had in the past, the principal of the loan would drop faster with each payment. In a few months, he was out from under the "upside-down" credit problem.

Jerry learned not to loan his credit or credit cards to people, even though he could trust them to pay back the debt on time. He also learned to shop for the best credit card rates and be more selective.

★   ★   ★

IT IS IMPORTANT TO BE DEBT FREE

Most American consumers use some form of debt:

$ Credit cards

$ Department store credit cards

$ Cash advances

$ Personal loans

$ Collateralized loans, such as auto or mortgage loans

COLLATERALIZED means that you are taking something you own and you use it as collateral for the loan. If you do not pay back the loan, the item is taken in exchange for nonpayment of the loan. This will damage your credit record. It is much better to pay the loan.

It is not unusual to find a household that may have all of these forms of debt at one time. The majority of consumers can quickly find themselves so overwhelmed with their debts, they have no money left when they bring the paycheck home and pay the bills.

Credit can be a fabulous tool, but it can easily add up to a life of living only to pay the bills. This is not a good way to live. If you have NO debt, you probably have not yet established any credit. THERE IS NOTHING WRONG WITH THIS! If this is something you choose to do, you can establish credit fairly easily. But, once you have established your first piece of credit, be on your guard. The junk mail will arrive frequently and you may be enticed to get more than you want or need.

HOW TO ESTABLISH CREDIT

Establishing credit is easy. Controlling credit is challenging. When you are ready to establish credit, it's best to already have a checking and savings account with a bank for a period of six months or more. This will show you have a good working relationship with your bank.

Ask your bank for a small personal, collateralized loan, for example, $500.00, against your savings account. Pay it back, as determined by the loan agreement. Send payments a few days early. Add a few extra dollars to the minimum payment due to pay off the loan early. At the end of the term, you will have established your first piece of credit history. Congratulations!

Go through the process again. Before the end of your second term, you will begin to receive advertisements through the mail about credit cards and loans you may be eligible for. Be selective! Read the fine print! Credit cards and loans are becoming more complex every day. Your goal is to have a credit card with the lowest interest rate possible and no annual fee. The better your credit history, the better the offers that come through the mail.

CAUTION! Be sure that the advertisement has been sent from a bank, thrift, savings & loan, or a credit union. There has been a huge amount of fraud in the credit card business. Individuals can gain access to your personal information by creating a phony 'solicitation' to provide you with credit. Look at the advertisement very, very carefully.

RESEARCH

Go on the web, run a Google search and look up CreditKarma. Establish an account. You can track your credit and find the BEST credit cards for your rating.

HOW TO MANAGE CREDIT

Those of you who already have credit and are paying on bills every month should focus all of your energy to pay them off. Imagine what your life could be like, right now, if you had no debts. It can happen, even if you have a mortgage. If you could pay off your debt and learn to live on what you earn, you would be surprised how much you would save, every pay period, toward your retirement.

You have been frequently told what a wonderful tax writeoff you have by obtaining a thirty-year mortgage. The percentage of the tax return, in relation to the money you have paid out over the thirty years is very, very small. If you could keep more of your money, paying the tax would not be such a burden. Paying monthly on a large variety of debts IS THE HUGE BURDEN.

If you have debts right now, organize a list. Pay off the smallest ones first. Get them off your back!

Focus your attention to paying off ALL of your debt. You will not need to buy a car through a loan again. You will not need to use your credit cards, even in an emergency. You will not have to pay a monthly mortgage. You WILL know a freedom that most people will never experience. This goal is reachable when your savings has been established and your debts have been paid.

CREDIT TROUBLE

Some of you reading this book are experiencing extreme problems with your debts right now. You may have a ruined credit record, collection agencies calling your home or office, or you may be behind in your payments. There are services available to you. There are services that can guide you through the process of cleaning up the entire mess WITHOUT FILING FOR BANKRUPTCY.

> Visit the National Association of Credit Management's website for help: https://nacm.org/

Your Credit Report

Your credit report contains historical information about how much you borrowed and repaid. It is compiled by using facts provided by creditors and public records (such as court documents). Credit bureaus prepare the information for creditors, employers and others who can show they have a legitimate reason for requesting your credit background.

You should request a copy of your credit report to verify that the information contained is accurate. Go online to CreditKarma.com and sign up. If you find inaccuracies, you may contact the three most frequently used credit bureaus at:

1. Equifax
    Information Service Center
    P.O. Box 740241
    Atlanta, GA 30384-0241
    1-800-685-1111

2. Experian (formerly TRW)
    National Consumer Assistance Center
    P.O. Box 949
    Allen, TX 75013-0949
    1-888-397-3742

3. Trans Union
    Consumer Disclosure Center
    P.O. Box 390
    Springfield, PA 19064-0390

1-800-851-2674

CREDIT COUNSELING

If you are really in trouble, contact a debt counseling center right away.

America Family Debt Counseling Centers, Inc.
A non-profit organization
2495 B Market, P.O. Box 109
Tiffin, OH 44883
Phone: 419-448-1963

CCCA - Consumer Counseling Centers of America, Inc.
A non-profit educational and social service organization
Suite 900, South Building
601 Pennsylvania Ave., N.W.
Washington, D.C. 20004
202-637-4851

To Complete the chapter

1. Manage your debt by organizing what you owe.
2. Prioritize which creditor will be paid off first, second, etc. through accelerated payments - lowest to highest.
3. Follow this procedure for each creditor.

You now have a plan to live easier on the money you currently make.

CREDIT SUMMARY

You have learned how to establish credit for the first time. You have also learned that credit is a great tool, but it can be easily abused and that debts have to be paid. It benefits you to keep your debts as low as possible and to accelerate paying them off. You have also learned who to contact for a credit report and that there are services available to you if you should have credit trouble.

After finishing this chapter, you are ready to begin Chapter 12 – Build Your Reserves. You will learn how to manage your savings and your money will begin to work for you.

CHAPTER 12

Build Your Reserves

This chapter will teach you how to build and manage savings. There are guidelines explaining how and when to move money through the progression of greater interest-bearing accounts. Examples are provided to show how to follow the progress of interest earned and record the money added to accounts. Taxable and non-taxable options are briefly described. The retirement account, as an additional savings method is described at the end of this chapter.

Study 8

Bernard and Rachel lived together in a small, one bedroom apartment and both worked. Bernard and Rachel each made good salaries, but never considered saving money for the future. One day, they decided it was time to buy a house together. When asked how much cash they had to put down on the house, they could not come up with a working figure.

First, they had to get organized. Bernard had two checking accounts, two savings accounts, a 401-K plan through his job and some money he invested in the stock market. Rachel had one checking account, two savings accounts, and IRA (individual retirement account) and a money-market account through the bank.

Some accounts held a small amount of money, but others held thousands of dollars. When they assembled all the forms and located the current total for each account, Bernard and Rachel were able to quickly total the eleven accounts.

They decided not to include their checking accounts, stocks, 401-K and IRA accounts in the total. So, they added the savings and money market accounts to determine a total they could work with. They found they had a sizeable amount of money that could be put toward the down payment of a house.

★   ★   ★

THE PROCESS

The process of saving money and building emergency funds can seem slow. But, when you practice the lessons learned in the previous chapters, such as:

- Saving all loose change
- Saving all remaining money each week from the allowance
- Rounding up in the check ledger each time a check is written
- Rounding down in the check ledger each time a deposit is made

You WILL begin to see a steady increase in savings.

It is frustrating to have an emergency while in the process of saving towards your goals. And usually, there are several emergencies at once, where you need to gain access to cash fast. But, you will suffer less and gain more by having more money in reserve. It is far less difficult to borrow from yourself than it is to ask someone for the money or to get a loan, especially when you cannot afford to do so.

Another way to increase your reserve is to put any unexpected money into your savings account. Unexpected money is:

- Overtime earnings
- Commission from sales
- A gift in the form of cash or check
- A tax refund
- Any money received, but not previously entered in your monthly plan.

Put all of it into the savings account. Never spend this money before it is in the bank. There are many tax refunds spent before a single dollar is ever received.

MOVING MONEY

1. When cash in your home savings containers reach an amount greater than $100.00, take the extra money over $100.00 and open a savings account.
2. When your checking account buffer is over $500.00, move the extra money into your savings account.
3. When your personal savings account holds more than $2,500.00, learn about CDs (Certificates of

Deposit) and Money Market accounts. You can then start earning interest on your money.

4. Open the CD when you have $1,000.00 or more.

Your next step is to consider the options that a larger balance gives you. If you enjoy having your money work for you, then you will be ready to invest in your first mutual fund. The minimums on mutual funds can be as low as $500.00. The average minimum is from $1,000 to $5,000.

Mutual Funds have become a very popular way to invest by sharing the risk and the reward with other investors. There are thousands of mutual funds to choose from. The most difficult part of investing in mutual funds is deciding which one(s).

Money managers receive a fee for handling the mutual fund. Some fee-paying methods are:

1. No load – No fees
2. Front load – A fee when you open the account
3. End load – A fee when you close the account
4. Load – A fee when you open and close the account

Annual or monthly service fees.

THE TREASURE CHEST

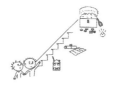

Keep all of your accounts organized. Record all appropriate facts about each account. Especially track the amount of interest you are earning.

RECOMMENDATION: Begin to read "Money Magazine." This will assist you in understanding the terminology, how to manage accounts and how to make sound financial decisions. Comparisons between loan interest rates, savings, CDs and Mutual Fund returns are found in this publication every month. It is written for the average consumer and will take you through other families financial situations. "Money Magazine" takes 3 or 4 sample households per month and assists them in organizing and developing financial plans. You can learn from other people's mistakes. It is less expensive this way.

401-K OR RETIREMENT SAVINGS PLAN

If you are offered a 401-K or Retirement Savings Plan through your place of employment, then SIGN UP! Choose the Aggressive plan while you are young. This is the best resource to save toward your retirement. You can usually choose how much you want to contribute and it is automatically deducted from each paycheck. I recommend the ROTH 401-K, as you will not pay capital gains tax when you go to pull this money out.

Having a savings account is wonderful. Having several accounts is better. Watching your money grow is great!

CHAPTER 13

The Best Things are Free!

GET A FREE EDUCATION

In the state of California, you can get a free college education by going to a community college. You will need to show proof of residency for at least two years. You will need to pay for books, labs and uniforms as needed. But, tuition costs are waived.

If you choose to study independently, there is a website known as OpenCulture.com that you should become familiar with. From their website, it lists the following available for FREE...

1300 Free online courses
150 Free Business courses
1000+ MOOC (Massive Open Online Courses).
200 Free Textbooks
300 Free Language Lessons
1,150 Free Movies
700 Free Audio Books
800 Free E-Books
Free K-12 Education

I encourage you to research these opportunities BEFORE spending money.

GET A BETTER PAYING JOB

There are over 75 of the BEST temporary job placement agencies listed on this site.

https://www.betterteam.com/staffing-agencies

START A SMALL BUSINESS

Starting a small business gives you a second stream of income. If you are working and not able to save what you should, start a business with some of your savings to get you to meet your financial goals much more quickly.

My advice is to do this on your own – meaning – do NOT borrow money to do this, if you can avoid it. My husband and I started A-Designs Audio, Inc. – a professional audio recording equipment manufacturer 20 years ago by investing $200.00 in a very tiny product. Once we sold out of the original product, we reinvested all the money into building and creating our second product. It was amazing to see the money grow.

I took on the bookkeeping and accounting, Peter took on the public relations, advertising, engineering, vendors and orders. We both continued working our day jobs until one day we realized we had enough saved to have Peter quit and work the business full-time, I quit my job after working for over 30 years for Mr. Michael Milken as his research librarian.

TAX SAVINGS

We all live with the pain of having taxes withheld from our paychecks. But, starting and running a small business gives us tax benefits. The deductions are many and varied, and they help us to keep more of our hard earned cash.

Some deductions include:

- Manufacturing costs - parts, metal, paint & silkscreen
- Printing
- Entertainment - dining out
- Legal
- Accounting
- Rent or Mortgage
- Utilities

And that's just to name a few.

If you are struggling with an idea - or don't know how to get started, I recommend finding a free counselor through the SBA's SCORE (Service Corp for Retired Executives).

"Score volunteers work with the SBA to provide small business mentoring and training to entrepreneurs through SBA offices." The homepage at SCORE.ORG has a link to: Find a Mentor or Find a Location. Through SCORE, there is no reason why you cannot get started today.

TRADING STOCKS

I Recommend starting an account with Charles Schwab. They offer checking, savings and brokerage firm accounts. Learn about day trading.

Example: TESLA

Buy low, sell high – repeat.

Place an order: When Tesla reaches $512, Buy.
When Tesla reaches $600, sell.
When Tesla reaches $592, buy.
When Tesla reaches $625, sell.
You might also want to try Disney, Amazon and EBAY.

Look at the stock history. What were the lowest and highest prices in 30 days? This is the range to place your buy/sell orders. Such a simple strategy.

HEALTH

Nothing is more important than your health. If you have CANCER - I can recommend you visit: CANCERTUTOR. ORG and learn how to take care of yourself.

I would like to recommend you purchase "Cure for All Diseases" by Hulda Clark, New Century Press, $19.99 – available through Amazon.com.

Learn as much as you can about Colloidal Silver form Steve Barwick, journalist with the Natural Health Journal. Colloidal Silver is available from Sprouts.

Please take care of yourself.

CONCLUSION

You have just completed an important learning journey. You have learned that having money, keeping it and saving it requires your attention. You have gained a better understanding of how you live and work with your money. You now have the basic tools needed to control what happens to your money instead of it controlling you.

DO NOT GET DISCOURAGED if you make a bad financial judgement, a mistake or if you spend 'foolishly.' Get up, dust yourself off and start again. It is not the end of the world. Like everything else in life, it takes practice to become a good money manager. Renew the process and get started. Don't give up. JUST DO IT!

It is your money and everybody wants a piece of it. Protect it by giving yourself the time to learn everything you can about managing your money. This knowledge will enable you to get what you deserve: To have, save and spend your money anyway you see fit.

Printed in the United States
By Bookmasters